Fatherhood Is a Verb

Also by Quintin Prout

POETRY

Nobe's Kitchen

Fatherhood Is a Verb

Quintin Prout

Copper Beech Press
Providence

Grateful acknowledgement is made to Randy Blasing, Samantha McCormack, Irina Abramov, Alyson Marzini, and Jason Marzini for their editorial eyes as first readers.

Cover art: "Errata Corrige" by Ekaterina Panikanova

Copyright © 2020 by Quintin Prout

All rights reserved.
For information, address the publisher:
Copper Beech Press
POB 2578
Providence, RI 02906
www.copperbeechpress@yahoo.com

ISBN: 13: 9780914278887

Set in Sabon
Printed by Stillwater River Publications
Manufactured in the United States of America
First Edition

For my daughter, Jahna

CONTENTS

Gender Class   11

I.

Across the Universe   15
"To the Moon, Alice!"   16
Meditations in an Emergency   17
Trumpet Starts   18
Bullied by Jazz   19
The Quiet Corner   20
Deficiency Slips   21
Jacob Wrestles with the A in Angel   22
Isaac Tells It   23
Lazarus in Pawtucket   24
Distilling Ghosts   25
Michael Grabs at Sunbeams   26
What Is a Straight Line For?   27
The Emperor of Swears   28
Creatures in Deep Soil   29
Chalk   30
Origin Story   31
Let the Feet Go Tramp   32
"God, When a Poem Finds You"   33
Poem-Making   34
Markings   35
Superhero Patterns   37

II.

Fatherhood Is a Verb   41
My Father Like Most   42
Employment   43
Nicknames from the Fishermen's Bar   44
Snarls   46
Drown   47
Done Gone   48
Midlife Crisis   49
The Water Cure   50
Approaching Twelve   51
Dead Letter Blues   52
Map   54
Wheels for Trees   55
Agree to Disagree   56
At Paper Nautilus   57
Like When You Count Between Thunder & Lightning   58
To Bounty Mama's Belly   59
Kissing Birch   60
The Comfort of Strangers   61
Toy Store in a Blackout   62
In the Margins   64
Above Giants   65
Beta Testing the Apocalypse   67

Fatherhood Is a Verb

GENDER CLASS

Despite the facts—
My face full

Of beard
And mustache.

Even though
I've fathered

A daughter
And been addressed

As *uncle*
For years.

This room
And its tiny

Occupants
Emasculates me:

Ms. Quintin,
I need the bathroom.

Ms. Quintin,
More glue—

(Monday to Friday
& year-round)

Ms. Quintin,
Q is for you.

Ms. Quintin,
Your dreads so long!

Tomorrow's letter of the day
Will be "A,"

For the A-line dress
They can see adorning me.

I

*Children know they are each different
in style and story.*

VIVIAN GUSSIN PALEY

ACROSS THE UNIVERSE

Each noon
It all shuts down:
Sixteen children
Make for thirty-two eyes
Slowly closing
Under a lullabied
Rendition of Lennon's
Cosmic Buddhist quest.
Their mesh cots a grid
To follow across
The hours of naptime
That unfold
Along the outposts
Of the learning space
I hold for them.

"TO THE MOON, ALICE!"

When asked
What made me angry,
My Pre-K self said,

"I just want to go
To the moon!"

"The trip there is
A long one,"
Teacher replied,

"And bad boys aren't
Allowed on its surface.

When you get back,
You'll be old
And your family

Won't recognize you,
Old and gray, still

Behaving this way.
See for yourself:
The moon isn't

Smiling."

MEDITATIONS IN AN EMERGENCY

after Frank O'Hara

In the chaos
Of the afternoon

That as a teacher
I'd lost control of,

He sat
Alone on the circle rug,

The soles of his feet
Touching, arms down,

Palms up—
Jeremiah in eternal

O.K.

TRUMPET STARTS

We form a N'Orleans 2nd line
At circle time, just behind our
Teacher's impromptu parade.
He blows into the brass,
& we echo—what comes out
The bell. Our handmade
Instruments held together
By white glue & glitter,
Except for Effie's
Real-to-life recorder.
She plays assured of her feats
& we believe the shouts & jubilee.
'Cuz she's older, 'cuz she knows
The balance of Dixieland and wonder.

BULLIED BY JAZZ

For me, the word "jazz" means, "I dare you."
                                    Wayne Shorter

Randy Weston's "Sweet Meat"
Triggered it all, even
Before a note was played
On Rhodes—

His composition written
In the seventies
Shared my bullied
Name in the eighties.

I hadn't even noticed
Any of the solos
But recalled the lone
Pathways through

Tunnels in the basement
I took by the gym, to avoid
An ass-kickin'—
Could those be jazz?

Could my improvised
Escape routes as a boy
Be notated on a staff
And called a *song?*

THE QUIET CORNER

I need a moment
To collect myself.

Limbs broken off,
Flapping,

As I try
To re-attach them.

Rolling my torso
To the corner—oh,

Dumb dough
That's been gone

Too long, and kids
Always notice.

So tomorrow
I'll try again

To recognize myself
And the name

They say that's right
In front of me.

DEFICIENCY SLIPS

By the end
Of the day, I'd
Collected one
For each class.

And the word
Was out—

They felt as big
As poster boards,
And I had
To carry six

Of them home
To return the next day,

Parent-signed.

*

Boxes checked off.

My name
Beside words
Too extreme to

Sound out
But meaning

Failure.

JACOB WRESTLES WITH THE *A* IN *ANGEL*

And I tend
To remember
The ones
Who struggle
With words—
Young wrestlers
With the alphabet,
Fearless, patient
With the slops
Of writing,
And brave
When their
Tongues
Suddenly
Crash.

ISAAC TELLS IT

Flame

Came hiding in
The wall, until

We fell asleep.
He's a cheater, and

His game is unfair,
And I know

All the ways
To play—

Smoke isn't much
Better.

Together they
Bullied our house

To nothing; my
Five birthdays

Burned down to ash.

LAZARUS IN PAWTUCKET

1
The Easter bunny looks moth-eaten
And the children want
No part of him.

Not even the photographer's
Charlie McCarthy doll speaks
To them—

And he's been doing this
Laughter thing
For years.

2
Still no takers.
No one sits
On his knee—

And the children
Are questioning,
Their beliefs.

3
But parents insist
On proof—

Stay clean. Don't play.
Smile. Be perfect.

Have faith.

DISTILLING GHOSTS

for Gwendolyn Brooks

They continue
To name children
After whiskeys:

Bourbon boys, little
Bourbon girls,

Who are actually
Quite lucky
To carry around two

Beautiful spirits, among
Us single-souled

Believers.

MICHAEL GRABS AT SUNBEAMS

It forms a perfect cylinder
Just above him—

A light-saber he wants
To "Show & Tell."

But it's just a window shade
Pretending to be a door

Letting his tomorrows
In.

WHAT IS A STRAIGHT LINE FOR?

This is going
To get uncomfortable.

Ten paces into
Our walk outside,

It's whispered
Down the line.

Don't worry.
I won't repeat it

Here on the page
Or at poetry readings.

But why this formation?
Why has he chosen

This time to share
With schoolmates

Things brought up
By his mother's tongue:

Inappropriate.
Erect.

THE EMPEROR OF SWEARS

That "Mother-fucker" still
Hangs over the schoolyard
Weeks later.

A "Niggah" fog
Coating molasses oil-
Thickness on

Apparatus meant
For fun, laughter,
Juvenile joy.

But that
"Mother-fucker"
Won't let us be—

Every recess, we gawk
At the point of origin,
As if the emperor of swears

Was still there, standing
On his soapbox,
Letting the world know

This learning "Shit"
Jus' ain't
Right.

CREATURES IN DEEP SOIL

The seed box explodes
From our hands,

So that we no longer
Know what's what.

Last year sunflowers,
Cucumbers, and tomatoes

Grew in our city garden.
But this season we'll just

Have to wait, water,
And wait some more—

You're convinced
They'll mutate,

And a new strain
Half-vegetable, half-

Flower will bloom. So
We wait—and water

The horror show
To come.

CHALK

The art is missing!
And everything's
Been restored—

To its colorless state.
Smears, hints
At arm movements,

And hands dusted
With pigments
Of echoes guessed

To be the ghosts
Of yesterday's
Creative outbursts.

Children point
At the sky,
Trying to fathom

The amount of rain
It takes to wash
Young dreams away.

ORIGIN STORY

At play,
The child

I remember
Must've

Tripped over
Or somehow

Broken open
A golden fragile

Thing
In the brain

That began,
Began again,

A daily
Blooming

So bountiful,
So many-hued.

LET THE FEET GO TRAMP

after a pre-war skipping song

Live a little. Become
Train song. Imagine
A world beyond your
Limited playground.
Go ahead. They ain't
Watching and I won't tell.
Here, let me guide you
Into a dance can't no
Music support. Leave
Your sensibilities. Leave
This self you think
You know so well—
Look down the tracks,
Ain't that a new you
Tramping this way?

"GOD, WHEN A POEM FINDS YOU"

At fifteen I wrote that
Single line
To God—

No other
Pronouncements,
No clues

To my newfound
Glory.
Maybe I thought

To prepare him
For something
He'd taken

For granted,
Some enlightenment
I thought

He knew nothing
About.

POEM-MAKING

for my students

Gather the letters around you.
Stop any in-fighting among them.

Pose a question. Allow for some play—
Words will form, then riches.

Then parts of you you must give
Away.

MARKINGS

after Seamus Heaney

1
Streetlights seem
Sadder now. Their
Posts no longer mark

A proud placement,
No longer the timekeepers
Of our childhood games.

Now just tack boards
For torn announcements,
Their time long passed.

2
Luminosity
Hung like a doo-wop group

Made up of aunties
On a stoop

In a neighborhood,
Lit every hundred feet.

3
It's an effort
To remember
My brothers,
Cousins, and friends
Under those lamps
In another time,
Doin' all sorts
Of things.

4
Cyclops!
Then another
On the odd-numbered
Side of the street.

All-important
To our summers,
They played
Our monsters

And protectors
Both.

SUPERHERO PATTERNS

Papa let me wear
A skirt today,

But with pants
Underneath.

We spent breakfast
Talking about what

The others might say
Or do.

I'm fearless in patterns
Of blue against red,

A Supergirl
They've never seen.

"Look, up in the sky!"
Papa jokes.

And I know it's because
He's nervous for me;

His boy's first day
Of kindergarten

Should be, and is,
All about

Heroes.

II

Everything parents us.
JONTERRI GADSON

FATHERHOOD IS A VERB

for Roman-Jahn

Nouns have been misused.
Handled so poorly
They no longer
Believe in our existence.
Black papa-ghosts
Haunt the childhoods
Of historians & filmmakers
Who try to conjure up
The vanishings—
When, in actuality, here
We are *reading* to sons
And daughters about this,
Our so-called phantom
Stillness.

MY FATHER LIKE MOST

Like most anglers, my father
Protected his remote fishing spots,
But not for the reasons I thought—
Not because of the wealth of bass
Or blues that schooled in
Unheard-of numbers. Where he
Could walk, if he wanted,
Across their slick backs, mid-ocean,
And deposit them straight into
His bucket, net-free. No, he held
Tight those locations because of
Their silences—the in-between
Moments where he'd mumble
A prayer or a good-luck shanty,
His *Leroy* time: quietly working
The thinnest lines, baiting hooks
With just the right amount
Of deep desire. Reading and rereading
The tides and the waves—the waves
Around him. Isn't casting out
And reeling in the work of writers?
Isn't his spirit still there, offshore,
In the throes of poetry?

EMPLOYMENT

When I'm unemployed, I
Don't write, even though
Hours expect me to.

It's the downtime of jobs
That employs me to create,
Like winters in an ice-cream café.

Or like today, while Pre-K
Sleeps, I'll steal away
The time to float

Between murmurs and poems
That will never earn
A living wage.

NICKNAMES FROM THE FISHERMEN'S BAR

1. "Footman"

Still smells like night-crawlers
Hooked for the first time
On steel and line—
His pole always danced
And his fish always
Seemed happy to be
Caught.

2. "Gorilla"

Myth says you
Were there:
The clubhouse,
A pool cue, coma.
With a name so mighty
You still hadn't
The strength to help
My father, who slept
Inside himself for weeks
And woke a new papa
I had to get
To know.

3. "Captain Hook"

Late afternoons into
Early evenings, I
Was always at the bar.

Maybe ten years old.
Maybe seven.

He offered me Luden's
Wild Cherry cough drops
Like candy—his claw

Pinching quarters
Into a pinball machine,
While deckhands cheered

Another round!

SNARLS

I can no longer free
The knots
From her hair.

I needn't braid or
Help in any ritual

I've come to know
As fatherhood—
She sets the table

& clears it after
We're done.

Tomorrow's clothes
Already laid out,
Lunch made.

I'm the only thing
In the house

Disheveled.

DROWN

When I stopped writing poetry
My basement flooded.

That's not a metaphor,
It's a fact—the basement

Of my childhood home,
To be exact. Water

Claimed the entire
Poetic library I'd

Boxed up months before
My departure. Humbled,

I returned to a flood—
And Mama watched

From the third floor as I,
The son who'd given up

Living with her, given up *breathing*,
Tried to save it all.

DONE GONE

Poetry has departed

In quest of a more
Deserving pen.

I can barely see it
Running down

Ether Street, looking
For an exit.

To the airport?
Because it's ready

For flights, arrivals,
Outer space, even,

Off among galaxies
Stretching farther

Than any satellite's reach.

MIDLIFE CRISIS

Until I feared I would lose it, I never loved to read.
                                                    Scout Finch

Maybe you're the type
To buy a shiny fast car,
Or someone who'll

Sit alone, feverishly
Consuming an ever-
Growing stack of books.

Either way, you're speeding
Towards something that
Doesn't give a damn about

Checkered flags or how
Well-read you're dying
To be.

THE WATER CURE

She led me back to words.
Wet footprints
On the hardwood floor
Traced the speed
Of her tiny feet.
My first instinct was
To worry about injury
As, towel in tow,
Our daughter ran
From the shower
To write something down
She didn't trust herself
To remember, her droplets
A trail returning me
To the urgency of verse.

APPROACHING TWELVE

She pens her first memoir,
As required by middle-school
English, a reflection on loss.
There are cherry blossoms.
There is a grandmother, great.
Great. She is younger than
I was when I began to place
Words in poetic order; she hears
The tiniest notes of memory,
Putting a slow, precise finger down
On midnight's resonant key.

DEAD LETTER BLUES

1
Some years
After his passing,
A post-marked
Envelope came
For me.

Inside were
Four folded,
Typed pages
Of verse.
The author?

My father,
His name
In cursive.

2
I recognized
The imperfect keys
And mis-shapen *E*'s
That also marked
My early work.

Our fingers
Had labored on
The same machine.
I was fifteen,
Maybe he was sixty,

Never mentioning
His nights of poetry.

3
Dear Cousin,

Thought you
Might want these.

Didn't know
Uncle Leroy wrote.

Never saw him
With a book.

Just his 18-wheeler
And Scotch.

Still writing?
Been thinking:

Maybe I'll start.

MAP

Our daughter asked
For locations—

A map shop,
And she cleared

A spot, on her
Bedroom wall,

For placement,
To plot out cousins

Or kin globally,
Connecting all points

With a red string:
Topography as

Blood instrument
To strum—to compose

Love on.

WHEELS FOR TREES

From the pantry window
My daughter questions,
Wheels on trees?

She leans out between
Curtains pinned back theatrically—
It all seems in miniature,

As I approach the slow bark
Of her mystery: the metal-
Spoked, tireless rim

That once held a clothesline
But now is just *time* compressed
To a rusted finger also pointing.

At her age, I hung the wash carefully,
As not to drop the garments
Still wet-heavy in weather.

They always returned, I tell her,
Warmed by summer—
Modernity in the wind.

AGREE TO DISAGREE

I place dots in the indexes
Of poetry collections

Next to poems I
Admire or envy.

My daughter thumbs
Through a volume

Among the stacks on
The dining room table;

I'm cooking. She calls
To me, asking about

My notations and
Begins to read.

Grunt to groan—she
Disagrees with my choices

And reaches for a pencil
To mark down her own.

AT PAPER NAUTILUS

She sang uncontrollably
Throughout the stacks—

Full-voiced or as full
As a five-year-old could get.

Doesn't she know it's Sunday?
A church day, my Zen

And bookstore-hopping day.
Yet she catches

My angered heart
When she rhymes *book*

With the *nook*
She now reads in.

LIKE WHEN YOU COUNT BETWEEN THUNDER & LIGHTNING

With each breath
I write a sentence
Until her next cough.
Silence—
Another line.
Breath, wait?
One more word, then
"Cough!"
She's trying
To sleep, I'm trying
To poem—us
Poor things.

TO BOUNTY MAMA'S BELLY

Every night you dance
On scallop shells that
Form an unknown
Mosaic.

Each morning you wake
Surrounded by black tea
Bags and clay; your
Afternoons

Are spent inventing words
And gathering faith
In their new
Meanings.

You're ten yet sure
Of these routines, sure
Siblings can be
Conjured straight

Out of dreams.

KISSING BIRCH

A five-foot branch
Bears the weight
On the left side of the arch
That separates our
Double living room;
Thankful for being saved
From the wood chipper
On the church lawn.
And as I lean in
For a writer's ritual
Kiss, my daughter
Eyebrows the moment,
Suspecting poems come
From birch, whispering
Sanctified in
Her papa's ear.

THE COMFORT OF STRANGERS

She just wants to sleep among
The books in the front room,

On a school night, with all the bards
And painters framed—I try to lullaby her

But she's way ahead of me.
Locked in private conversations

And the comforts of learning
Strange names and the titles

That surround her. Tonight
I'm not invited. Tonight,

Others guide her growth.

TOY STORE IN A BLACKOUT

1
And four days
Before Christmas,
With just our cellphone
Flashlights to locate joy.
We moved as outlines
Of ourselves. Spot-lit
Here. No, *here*—
Bumping into other
Anxious bodies desperate
To discover just the right
Degree of happiness—
To shine through
And wrap up all
At once.

2
In darkness she thought
They'd come to life,
Moving between the beams
Of light: *Look, Papa!*
Every inanimate thing: *Look!*
There! Papa, can't you see?

3
From the sidewalk,
It mimicked a looting—
Half the East Side cloaked
And pulling items
From shelves—*A holiday?*
Bystanders will ask,
Unaware of the caroling
Inside.

4
Driving away,
All of us parents
Knew that no gift
That year would thrill
Or remain as fresh
In their minds
As that evening:
That evening!
They'll say,
Lamenting
As adults.

IN THE MARGINS

I'm forced to write
This poem

On the end pages
Of my daughter's

Dr. Seuss book—
Pen beside me

But no paper, only this
Leftover space

To the right of a library
Card. "Oops!"

I laugh—
But do not disturb her:

Eyes closed, face up
Towards my chin,

Arms twitching
At times,

As if her brain
Is still trying

To catch rhymes.

ABOVE GIANTS

1
Podium full—
In our neighborhood's
Last independent
Bookstore.

All the poets mic'd
As she—*tiny*—enters
The door to
What is now her

Applause.

2
A purposeful child,
I would say,
but barely saw—

Just heard the type
Of high-steppin'
That upstages

Words.

3
Everyone's distracted!
Poems stumble over
Their meanings, like
A speaker's feedback.

The buzz on all our tongues
Asking—
What book has that
Little one come for?

Of all the writers present,
Who's her chosen one?

4
On her giant's shoulders
She's already in love

With the books purchased
And, to the authors below,

Waves.

BETA TESTING THE APOCALYPSE

1
Breaking news!
She texted,

Followed by
No school!

Virus?
I replied.

Her thumbs-up
Emoji—

Apologetic,
She typed:

*Papa, I'm not that
Happy.*

2
As the numbers rise,
We brace for the worst
Week, *this* week,
And prepare our
Next read in isolation:

A graphic novel about
The end of the world,
We presume, because
Of its title and the men
In white coats on the cover

Signifying the distance
Between her and me
And the disease.

3
I post paintings & poetry
On social media for friends
And loved ones locked down,
Bored, or feverish.

Tonight I ask her
To choose an artist
To present and a writer
For tomorrow—

I love talking to her
About tomorrows.

www.ingramcontent.com/pod-product-compliance
Lightning Source LLC
LaVergne TN
LVHW042000060526
838200LV00041B/1803